My First NFL Book

NEW ORLEANS SAINTS

Nate Cohn

LET'S READ
AV2 BY WEIGL
ADDED VALUE • AUDIO VISUAL

www.av2books.com

LET'S READ
AV²
BY WEIGL™
ADDED VALUE • AUDIO VISUAL

Go to **www.av2books.com**, and enter this book's unique code.

BOOK CODE

D589264

AV² by Weigl brings you media enhanced books that support active learning.

AV² provides enriched content that supplements and complements this book. Weigl's AV² books strive to create inspired learning and engage young minds in a total learning experience.

Your AV² Media Enhanced books come alive with...

Audio
Listen to sections of the book read aloud.

Video
Watch informative video clips.

Embedded Weblinks
Gain additional information for research.

Try This!
Complete activities and hands-on experiments.

Key Words
Study vocabulary, and complete a matching word activity.

Quizzes
Test your knowledge.

Slide Show
View images and captions, and prepare a presentation.

... and much, much more!

Published by AV² by Weigl
350 5th Avenue, 59th Floor
New York, NY 10118

Website: www.av2books.com

Library of Congress Control Number: 2017930769

ISBN 978-1-4896-5529-5 (hardcover)
ISBN 978-1-4896-5531-8 (multi-user eBook)

Printed in the United States of America in Brainerd, Minnesota
1 2 3 4 5 6 7 8 9 0 21 20 19 18 17

042017
020317

Editor: Katie Gillespie
Art Director: Terry Paulhus

Weigl acknowledges Getty Images and iStock as the primary image suppliers for this title.

My First NFL Book

NEW ORLEANS SAINTS

CONTENTS

2 AV^2 Book Code
4 Team History
6 The Stadium
8 Team Spirit
10 The Jerseys
12 The Helmet
14 The Coach
16 Player Positions
18 Star Player
19 Famous Player
20 Team Records
22 By the Numbers
24 Quiz/Log on to
www.av2books.com

Team History

The New Orleans Saints joined the NFL in 1967. Their city was nearly destroyed by a hurricane in 2005. The team's success after the storm lifted the city's spirits. The Saints became one of the best teams in the NFL after that.

The Saints had to borrow stadiums in other states after the storm hit.

4

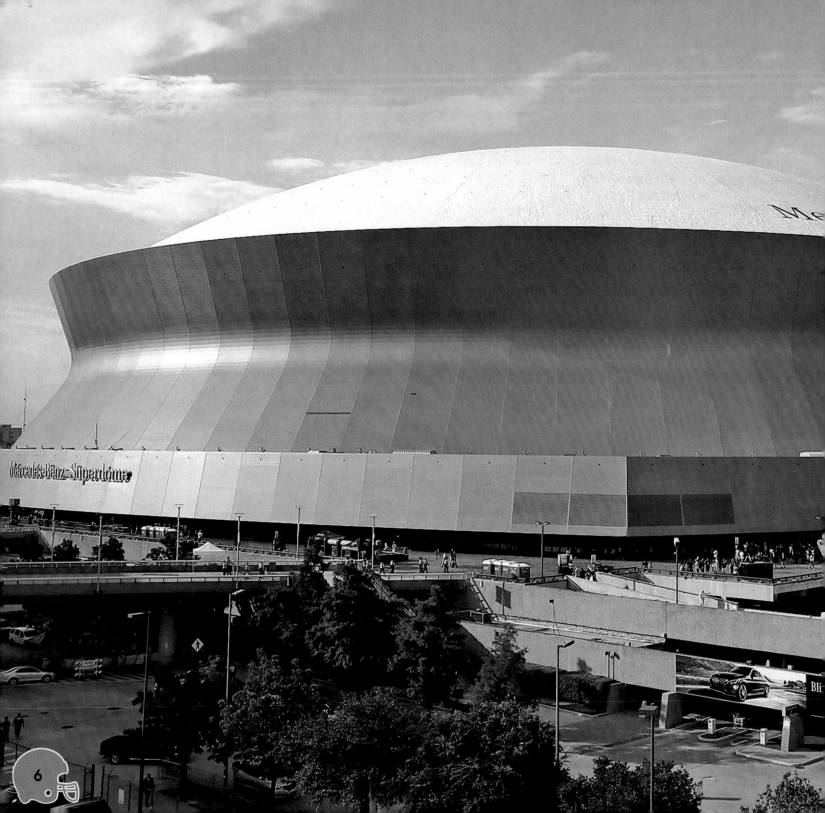

The Stadium

The Saints play at the Mercedes-Benz Superdome. The Superdome opened in 1975. This stadium was closed for repairs after the big storm in 2005. It opened again the next year. The Superdome has hosted seven Super Bowls.

The Mercedes-Benz Superdome is in downtown New Orleans, Louisiana.

Team Spirit

The Saints' mascots are Sir Saint and Gumbo. Sir Saint is a cartoon football player with a very large chin. Gumbo is a cartoon dog in a Saints uniform. The name "Gumbo" comes from a kind of soup that is popular in New Orleans.

Gumbo looks like a kind of dog called a Saint Bernard.

The Jerseys

The Saints' colors are black and gold. The gold they use is shiny like metal. The team wears black jerseys with gold numbers for home games. The Saints marked their 50th season in 2016. They added a patch with the number 50 to the front of their jerseys that year.

The Helmet

The Saints' helmets are gold with the team logo on each side. The logo is a shape called a fleur-de-lis. It was used by French kings and queens as a sign of power. New Orleans was settled by French people long ago.

The word *fleur* is French for "flower."

13

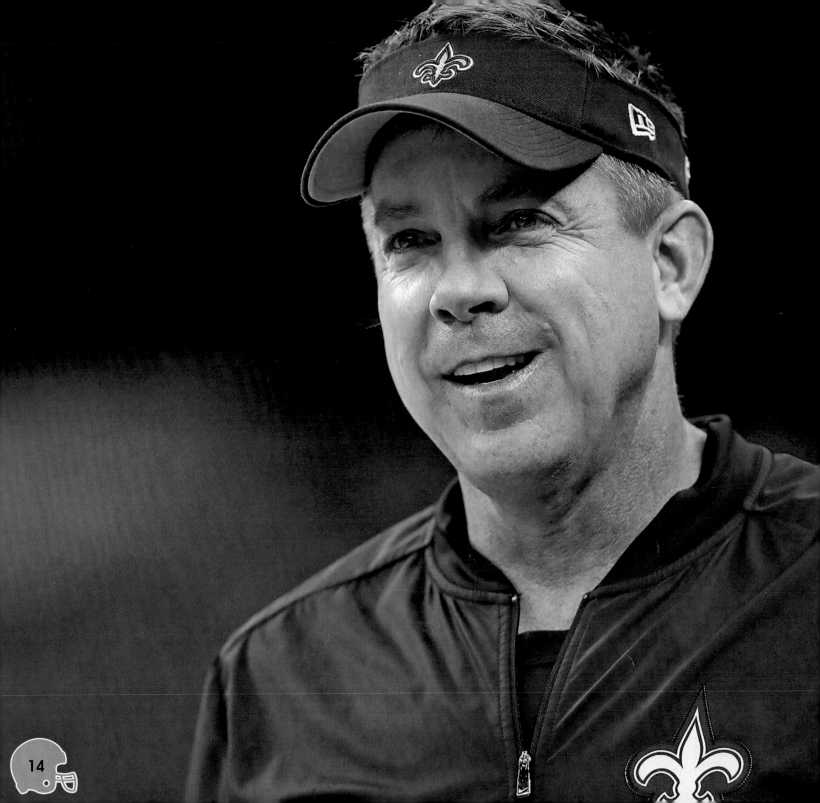

The Coach

Sean Payton is the Saints' head coach. He led the Saints to a Super Bowl title for the 2009 season. Payton has been the team's coach since 2006. He was a backup quarterback in the NFL before becoming a coach. Backup quarterbacks follow each play called during games. This is good training for head coaching jobs.

Player Positions

Making a field goal takes two players. One player holds the ball. The other kicks it. The holder is sometimes the quarterback. Teams can "fake" field goals. They will line up as if they are going to kick. The holder then picks up the ball and passes it or runs with it.

The longest field goal in NFL history was 64 yards.

Star Player

Drew Brees joined the Saints in 2006. He has become one of the best quarterbacks in the NFL. Brees helped the team win a Super Bowl. He was named that game's Most Valuable Player. Brees has been to the Pro Bowl 10 times. That is the yearly game for the best NFL players.

Archie Manning was the Saints' quarterback from 1971 to 1982. He is in the Saints' Hall of Fame. Manning was known for "scrambling" to avoid defenders. This means he would run before passing the ball. Manning's sons Peyton and Eli also went on to be star NFL quarterbacks.

Team Records

The NFL is split into eight divisions. The Saints have made their division's playoffs five times since 2006. The playoff games decide who goes to the Super Bowl. The Saints have won one Super Bowl. The team's all-time leading scorer is Morten Andersen. This kicker made 1,318 points.

1 Super Bowl Win

5 Division Playoffs in 10 Years

Morten Andersen

1,318 Points

By the Numbers

Archie Manning went to the Pro Bowl **2 times** as a Saint.

The Saints won **10** games in 2006 to finish **1st** in their division.

Mercedes-Benz paid **$100 million** to put its name on the Superdome.

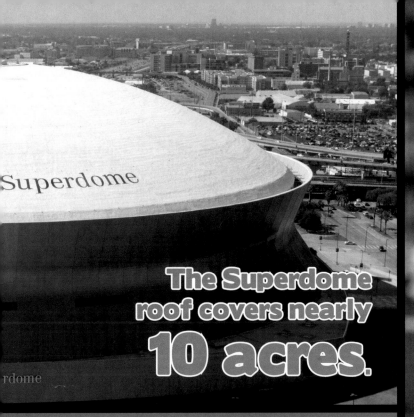

The Superdome
roof covers nearly
10 acres.

Drew Brees set
an NFL record
by throwing
touchdowns in
54
games in a row.

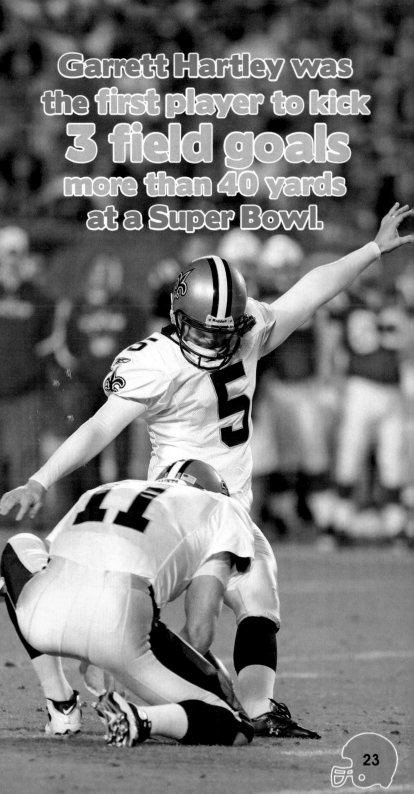

Garrett Hartley was
the first player to kick
3 field goals
more than 40 yards
at a Super Bowl.

Quiz

1. How many Super Bowls has the Mercedes-Benz Superdome hosted?

2. What kind of dog is Gumbo?

3. Who used the Saints' logo before the team did?

4. How many times has Drew Brees gone to the Pro Bowl?

5. What was Archie Manning known for doing to avoid defenders?

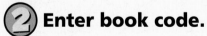